Elk in Winter

Previous books by Robert Pack

POETRY

Rounding It Out
Minding the Sun
Fathering the Map: New and Selected Later Poems
Before It Vanishes: A Packet for Professor Pagels
Clayfeld Rejoices, Clayfeld Laments: A Sequence of Poems
Faces in a Single Tree: A Cycle of Monologues
Waking to My Name: New and Selected Poems
Keeping Watch
Nothing But Light
Home From the Cemetery
Selected Poems (England)
Guarded by Women
A Stranger's Privilege
The Irony of Joy

POETRY FOR CHILDREN

The Forgotten Secret
Then What Did You Do?
How to Catch a Crocodile
The Octopus Who Wanted to Juggle

LITERARY CRITICISM

Belief and Uncertainty in the Poetry of Robert Frost
The Long View: Essays on the Discipline and Hope of Poetic Craft
Affirming Limits: Essays on Morality, Choice and Poetic Form
Wallace Stevens: An Approach to His Poetry and Thought

TRANSLATIONS (with Marjorie Lelash)

The Mozart Librettos

CONTENTS

Acknowledgments ix

1 *Place*

Late in the Rockies 3
October Larches 5
Deer at the Garden 6
Fire Season, 2000 8
Eagle 10
Full of Summer 12
White Horse 13
Harvest 15
Raven 16
The Darker Green 18
The Sea in the Trees 19
Elk in Winter 21
Elevation 24
Double Rainbow 25
Forms 27
Warmth 28

2 *Person*

Confession 33
Thirst 36

Twin Poem 39
Arrowhead 41
The Fan's Soliloquy 43
Picnic 45
Midsummer Music 48
Clone 51
Betrayal 54
Divorce 56
Journey 58
Returning 66
The Book 68
Two Jews on a Train 70
Evening Meditation 74
Evasion 78

3 *Perspective*

What Would Wind Say? 83
Distance 85
Faint Memory 87
Contentment 89
Molecular Celebration 91
The Ceiling 94
Go Jump 95
Marveling 97
Bounty 100
Distraction 102
Bullfrog Sonata 105
Reply of the Frog Princess 107
Remains 109
Defiance 111
Ripeness 113
Ghosts 116
Showdown 118

ACKNOWLEDGMENTS

The author wishes to thank the editors of the following periodicals for permission to reprint poems that first appeared in their pages:

American Press: "Deer at the Garden"
Poetry: "Eagle," "Arrowhead," "Distance," and "Remains"
Prairie Schooner: "The Fan's Soliloquy" and "Midsummer Music"
Raritan: "Late in the Rockies"

1

Place

LATE IN THE ROCKIES

Here in the Rockies as dark clouds descend,
Gray sky and snow upon the peaks contend and merge,
Partaking of each other's shadows in the lake
Where sleek ducks circle and then separate;
Their luminescent wings reflect

Bright breaks in the black clouds, and I forget
Why lately I moved here. In this new place
I can reflect on what I see in the still lake,
The reassembling ducks, called goldeneye, that merge
White wings with snowy sky, so I can't separate

These swirling whitenesses
Or tell this house from rooms I won't forget.
The whirling seasons merge
In just a single image in the lake—
The gold eye of a duck—which like gold sky

Between black clouds reflects
My eye as one still image on the lake.
And now I have no need to separate
Sorrows of empty doors I can't forget
From vistas darkening—all merge,

Merely by being gone, into a white glow
On a lake where rowing with my father
I reflect my rowing with my son,

For I forget which day is which;
I cannot separate lake shimmer

From gold light spans in the sky. And staring up
Between dark closing clouds, I can forget
Why I can't separate
Where we were coming from or rowing to—they merge,
Just as a duck's eye can reflect my own.

Now only the closed sky is home.
Ducks on the lake reflect themselves, and yet
Their shadows merge with doorway shadows
And with window glistenings
That I have still forgotten to forget.

OCTOBER LARCHES

Across the mountainside in evening sun
Golden October larches flare,
As if they could delay dark days to come,
Winter encroaching everywhere

My momentary mind can reach.
And in the lake, silent as brooding inwardness,
The larches now are doubled, each
With a true partner in itself,

A multiplying plenitude of one,
Repeated and repeating in my mind.
Reflecting on its own reflections, stunned
With bold illumination of a kind

Beyond what golden sunlit larches teach
Of how to face the all-dividing dark, I find
A multiplying plenitude of one
Across the mountainside in evening sun.

DEER AT THE GARDEN

Even asleep, I hear them stirring in the woods,
Restless like me, and hungry,
Their large ears alert to danger sounds, human
Or merely wind, though since there never is enough
To eat, they'll trample down my garden
And devour what's mine. True, they're just deer,

But when I watch their eyes I don't see deer
As creatures with no rights, enough
Of them already in the woods,
I see what they would feel if human
Understanding told them I was hungry,
That the purpose of a garden

Is to fence those out who failed to make a garden
Though their children, just like deer,
Through no fault of their own, also are hungry.
But I'm not to blame, and I reject that human
Sentiment, because there's not enough
Where many people live, the same as in the woods,

As fear too is the same within the woods
Or out, and since I can't help everyone, it's human
That I first take care my children not go hungry
And can sleep at ease within my garden,
Though they seem wary just like deer
When I gaze in their eyes. It's good enough

If I can keep them safe; it's good enough
If I can keep my garden
Flourishing while more and more gaunt deer
Keep coming from the woods,
And though their limpid eyes look human,
Don't blame me because they're hungry.

Don't blame me that people too go hungry
For there's only so much room within a garden
Whether filled with people or with deer,
Some must make do within the woods
Where there can never be enough,
Though knowing that can cause more human

Misery. Hungry at heart for there to be enough
In all those teeming gardens and lush woods—
Are we most human when we see ourselves as deer?

FIRE SEASON, 2000

   A dull, wan, puzzled look, human
And recognizable, showed in his eyes.
The baby black bear lay there with his paws
Professionally bandaged in the photo
Of his rescue. I won't let myself imagine
All the creatures trapped and then incinerated
In a million burning acres, worst in a bad century,
Here in Montana and neighboring Idaho.

      Whose fault—there's got to be someone at fault—
What other consolation do we have but blame?
Maybe the logging industry
For cutting down the largest ponderosa pines
And leaving the combustible dry brush;
Or maybe we should blame the government's
Short-sighted policy of slashing funds
For needed caretaking—like thinning forests
Of young lodgepoles and dense undergrowth
And making cleansing burns we can control,
Restoring to the soil much needed nitrogen
As Nature did before Mankind arrived.

      But maybe it's the drought that we should blame,
Not something we ourselves have caused,
But Nature, in another of its many moods,
Just doing what it does, impersonal,
Not retribution for our sinfulness

As when the flood wiped most of Mankind out.
Yet I suspect such versions of apocalypse
Contain a hidden wish and thus reveal
A failure to confront cosmic indifference—
A wish behind the fantasy of punishment,
Of water gathering or lunging fire
Fanned out across the valley by the wind,
That we are really in control,
Since if disaster has been caused by us,
Blessing, likewise, is also ours to choose.

    So let's get on with blaming Human failure
Not the drought, and not the fickle wind;
Let's seize upon Promethean blind hope,
Changing our anger into useful work,
So we can save both forests and our homes,
So ponderosa pines will thrive
And silent elk still make soft passage there,
If only we reform, as surely it's within
Our power of will and reasoning to do.

    And if, meanwhile, a puzzled bear
Is fated to endure the consequence
Of Nature's droughts or floods or flames,
We will assume, well, that's just how it is;
We'll bandage the poor thing, forget, and then
Get on with other things to do.
We have ourselves to care about, that's natural;
We cannot change things in a day.
And yet, as I look at those blackened trees,
That leafless landscape bleakly desolate,
How can I be indifferent to Nature's
Blameless, vast indifference without
Making it my own? The bears, I hear
Their seared flesh sizzling in the blazing night.

EAGLE

At dusk, I see an eagle's silhouette
Drifting around her distant nest,
And think how close to stark extinction
She has come, the ultimate defeat,
Contingent on some human whim

Or human greed that would usurp her space.
And yet she floats so seemingly serene
As if the tides of air were everything
That needed to be understood,
As if the whole accumulation

Of the past were now,
And now again, and now forevermore
About to be with nothing
Unfulfilled to long for, nothing
To regret. And without envy, only

With a kind of love because
She helps me almost to forget myself,
I watch her tilted wings glide off and lift,
Swooping in some smooth current
I assume she uses and takes pleasure in

Without the need to say how she enjoys
Herself to make joy true.
And so I listen to my thoughts take flight,

I watch a second silhouette
Give further depth and amplitude to space,

Circling as if their hidden nest
Were the sure center of the universe—
A universe with purpose
And unchanging permanence,
Complete by being only what it is.

And so I try to think myself released
From thinking of myself
By fixing on the eagles' dips and swerves
Around their nest, my mind filled with their forms,
The angles of their silhouettes, their curves.

FULL OF SUMMER

This is the full of summer, this is all
Bold bumblebees have always dreamed about;
This floating is my *rise* that has no *fall;*
This steadiness my *in* that has no *out.*
And this my body's happiness—the call
Persuading me to pause deep in *today*
As purple clover scents the swaying air
Bold bumblebees have always dreamed about.
I watch more ripeness ripening the way
A whirling orange blur of oriole
Blends with lake water blazing everywhere;
A hummingbird suspended at a rose
As if in mimic of the sun whose flare
Holds her eternal moment in my mind.
This is my *opening* that has no *close;*
This is my *now* with *then* now left behind
And icy wind a thought *thought* can forestall:
This is the full of summer, this is all.

WHITE HORSE

    There in the middle distance in a field
Surrounded by a sagging fence,
A white horse canters head-up with an ease
Suggesting that he thinks he's beautiful.
On the south border, stacked between two trees,
A year's supply of split wood waits,
And from the north a stream runs toward me
Where it feeds a large trout pond
In which the white horse is reflected
When he drinks, his neck bowed in an arc.
    From where I watch, among dark firs,
Upon an elevation of my own,
I see the streaking whiteness of the horse;
I see the Mission mountain range,
Its chiseled peaks across the broadened sky
Already glistening with early snow,
As if a theme had been expanded
To a magnitude beyond what meditation
Might have thought impossible.
    Let light, I say out loud to no one
But myself, illumination of the scene
And of my mind, become a theme
That out of need I make my own:
The white horse in the field, the vast white
Of the mountain range, the spawning pond
Now shimmering in midday sun

With white wings on its coasting ducks;
Let them reveal nothing but what they are,
Horse, mountain, pond, without purpose,
Without meaning, without hope; yet let them join
In one white theme because I will it so.
    Horse, mountaintop, the leaping trout,
All share the mirrored light as if
Their flashing whiteness can compose the scene,
Can gather it together so a horse,
Poised in the arc its bowed head makes,
Might mean more than in fact it does,
As if somehow translucent consciousness
Really were part of a design
In which the flow of undulating light,
Whiteness connecting everything I see,
Were not my own invention out of need.
        What need? What am I saying here
That does not falsify the scene itself
With hinting impositions of my own?
Only horse, mountain, pond, the silent ducks,
Each in its lone existence separate
From mine, actually dwell there,
And yet shared whiteness, which my mind
Construes as part of a design, shines forth
In this suspended moment when I can believe,
With that horse stationary in the field,
All whiteness in the world is beautiful.

HARVEST

And so I make myself at home at last
Among depleted fields, wan evergreens
Hunched ghostlike under snow—wherein
I see my image which now means

I still find meaning in chilled bleak remains,
In breath contending with blank sky,
In rhymes asserting my companionship
With dull, indifferent light. No doubt that's why

A harvest of relinquishing the past
Restores the late least hint of what remains
Yet to be lost, and why a solitary owl's
Fixed stare repeats what my cold mind contains.

I choose the growing bounty of things gone,
Sad light diffusing everywhere,
Vague faces reappear and merge, bestowing
Care on those no longer in my care.

I choose the growing bounty of things gone,
A harvest of relinquishing the past;
I still find meaning in chilled bleak remains,
And so I make myself at home at last.

RAVEN

Black, luminescent black, not black
Betokening black night or blacker death,
This raucous bird is bringer of broad day,
Expanding sunlight through sheer glistening,
Making brushed air feel more abundant
With his serial cacophonies.

Predator, scavenger, brute survivor,
And thus no less convincingly immortal
Than the fabled nightingale
Or less symbolic of harsh nature's grim design
Suggested by the grackle's strident squawk,
Raven is also the abiding muse

Of myth-makers: One story goes
That when the housewife, Earth,
Grew jealous of free birds and animals,
Mischievous Raven
Transformed himself into a wind-blown seed
So that tricked Earth, asleep and dreaming,

Breathed him in and in due time
Gave birth to him as her own baby boy.
When Raven had grown old enough to play,
He stole the sun Earth sullenly had hidden
In the cellar of her house
And rolled it out the wooden door.

When finally outside and free again,
He turned himself back into Raven as he was
And loosed the sun back to the sky—
From where Earth first had snatched it—
In order to restore the blessed light
To all the shivering and hungry animals.

And so black Raven still remains
The bird of light, buffoon of happiness,
Brother of my bleak mood when my bleak thoughts
Are black with personal decease,
Black with desire to expunge the sun
And bring down smothered peace on everyone.

THE DARKER GREEN

Dark green, and darker green—bleak, bleak,
Even in fertile autumn shade,
But good to fit my gloomy mood
A continent from you—with yet to come
More gloom before green dark can reach its peak
As it must do for everyone.

I call this forest gloom my own
Though it takes cause from your dark grief,
For I can't bring your straining breath relief
Or find relief myself in blame;
Old age, not care, has crushed you to the bone,
And gloom keeps every latitude the same.

The loneliness I know you face
Cannot be measured by my dark larch trees,
My bleak home, muted by the numbing ease
Of green's soft darkening so far
From you in my gloom's colder place.
Though it's still summer where you are,

Only bleak weather swirls your mind
With nothing left there to express
Except the gloom of your late emptiness—
Blank hope for what comes after life,
A green you know you'll never find
As daughter, lover, mother, wife.

THE SEA IN THE TREES

Usually still, sometimes the trees
Are lashed to uproar by wild mountain wind
In this larch forest underneath a roiling sky,
But what I hear is the dull echo of the sea
Piling upon itself, stomping the shore,

Which makes me shudder so that my stirred mind
Demands two scenes to dwell upon:
The thrashing sea not present in my sight,
And the contorted trees, like waves blown by the wind.
Here the torn sky swirls like the ocean

My twin brother sees, which opens as a surge of wind
Contrives a pathway for streaked golden light.
My mind whirls with the sway of swirling trees,
Yet I can spy my brother on the shore
As if my life were not enough, as if the sea

With all its flying foam and salty wind,
Its fractured shells strewn on the shore,
Suggested journeys to console my mind
For losing touch with him. Perhaps he pictures trees
With me beneath this stormy sky

Which looks like ocean water even as the clouds
Part for an instant when bare wind
Makes way for golden light, a pathway from the shore

Right through the lunging sea
That leads to my own house. But now my mind

Attends to the shrill noise of swaying trees,
Though I recall them absolutely still, the larch
In autumn when my autumn mind,
Ablaze in bronze, imagined sunlight fled the sky
And entered them, imagined wind

Had gone back to its home within the sea
And left my brother stranded on the beach,
Hearing the cry of trees that gathers to a roar,
Trying to read wild wind words in the air,
Sea riddles of debris on the scarred shore.

ELK IN WINTER

Laden with snow
    the moonlit high pines
Loom above their shadows
    in the undulating drifts,
And in the watcher's mind
    a strange serenity
Pervades the silence
    of the windless scene,
As if permanent winter seals the woods
    from further change
And sets the mood the watcher now
    considers his reward
For seeing rounded moonlit forms
    with luminescent curves
And sweeping shades of blue.
    As silence deepens
Into deeper thought, the watcher,
    unresistant to the spell
His watching adds to the still woods,
    hears footfalls softly
Crunching in the shadowed snow,
    step upon sure unhurried step,
As marching elk, perhaps a hundred
    in a staggered line,
Their nostrils smoking over glowing eyes,
    push through on an ancestral path

To where elk go in wintertime
    beyond the watcher's gaze.
The watcher sees the elk as a tableaux,
    held in abeyance in his mind,
Because he senses some vague correspondence
    in their unrushed passing
Through the shadows of the pines
    and his hushed witness to the scene,
As if he could be anyone who came upon
    tall elk in moonlight,
Moving beneath loose shades of evergreens.
    And yet the watcher must
Acknowledge that awareness
    of a half-formed wish
to dwell forever in his watcher's mood
    distracts him into reverie
And thus disturbs his merging
    with the moonlit atmosphere
So that the silver scene can have
    no correspondence to himself
Other than that strong stomping elk
    have somewhere else to go
And feel no haste in getting there.
    He ponders that the wish
To lose himself in thinking of the passing elk
    defeats its goal
By mirroring his roused and wishful self
    and thus revives the gloom
Of contemplating his own murmured life
    or what is left of it.
His life, his self-reflecting life,
    with children gone into another mist,
And parents having crossed
    the last shore of the roaring brink,

Is it too precious to be dwelt upon
    with all his ghosts now
Numbered in the name of loss?
    The shudder of that thought
Flows backwards and recedes, and now
    the last of the cascading elk,
In what had seemed an endless line,
    passes from view;
The watcher sees himself
    beneath a steadfast tree,
His face in moonlight almost featureless,
    despite its worn-out care,
And does not know how long in silence
    he's been standing there.

ELEVATION

Here at this elevation, I see daffodils,
Yellow and white, in sunlight and in shade,
Now blooming as their nature wills,
Choosing to be exactly as they're made

To be in their own rooted hearts.
But down let's guess four thousand feet below,
They're withered and dried up, with just bare parts
Of rigid stalks remaining. Fresh bright snow

Glows high up on the mountain peaks, so I can hold
All seasons for a moment in my mind,
From ruddy April buds to harvest gold—
As if eternity cannot be hard to find

Right where I am, right here before my eyes.
Though in the valley, summer drought now kills,
Though blank snow glare obliterates blue skies,
Here at this elevation, I see daffodils.

DOUBLE RAINBOW

    From north to south, almost as far
As I can see, a double rainbow in dark clouds
Spans the snow-sparkled mountain range,
Its yellow, purple, green, and red
More solid, more defined, than any
Memory or sentiment can bring to mind.
    A raven flies beneath the rainbow's arch,
Evoking Yahweh's enigmatic promise
That He wouldn't send another flood
To purge the earth, and I'm reminded
Of His lifting His initial prohibition
Against eating meat because He realized
Our species needed flesh to satisfy
Our all-consuming appetite.
    The dread of us in all the animals
Has marked us from our second chance
After the flood, and now I think of Abraham,
For whom the rainbow bond with Noah
Was replaced by Yahweh's grim insistence
Circumcision would inscribe His covenant
Upon the flinching body as before
It had on earth and in the misty sky.
    Despite such grisly warning,
Which the Holy Book sears on my brain,
Our long vicissitudes had just begun,
And soon reasons for suffering emerged:
In order to maintain that He was just,

We figured we were chosen to be punished
For our worshiping of graven idols,
Failing to abide by His commandments
That we rise above what we were made to be.
But what vain hope lay hidden there
In such harsh judgment of ourselves:
If we have been the cause of our despair,
Might we not be the source of our own cure?
    But standing here, far from Jerusalem,
With fresh guilt for my being safe,
As if among the first-born of my tribe,
I say that two millennia is long enough
To wait for some reprieve from punishment.
    From Spain to Russia to the camps
At Dachau, Belsen, Auschwitz, and Buchenwald,
Despised as if we drained out children's blood
To make our bread of freedom—demon fathers
Counting money in the night—by those
Who'd drive us, the remaining few,
Into the sea upon a tide of hate, I say,
As if such revelation should suffice,
"We only have one human fate to share."
    And I say also to the rainbow
In the swirling clouds, "Be nothing more
Than chance refraction of the spectral light,
Reversed and doubled on itself;
Be nothing more than random particles,
And I'll give thanks that you
Have no more claims to make on me,
That you are simply what you are:
A rainbow of reflections that still gives
Delight to me in the dark pause of rain
Before I learn what can or can't be kept
Of human laws and human promises."

FORMS

When I say *circle* I select the sun
As illustration, I select the moon;
I offer to expanding space this one
Plucked apple in my outstretched hand.

Or for variety, elliptical
Eggplant and pear also can please,
The streaked breast of the meadow lark,
The arch of flowing willow trees.

Look there—an indescribable
Meandering of butterflies
Descending to an oval pond that's full
Of luminescent lily pads!

And so I make each sight my own
By naming it according to a form without,
For turning inward to myself alone
There's only thought to think about.

WARMTH

    I feel descending autumn sun
warm on my flesh, my arms exposed
    to its bronze radiance,
as if some message from the source
    where messages originate
has been received and perfectly decoded
    to convey the meaning
that this balmy air is all the purpose
    that needs searching for.
And now, within this borderless, ripe now,
    the thought of warmth—
warmth as idea—enhances
    what flares right before my eyes:
this family of swallows,
    luminescent purple-green,
circling and swooping here
    beneath my eaves
where they and I have come to share a place
    that fits some memory of where
their kind and mine have been before.
    Like sunlight on my arms,
this thought too touches me, its flow
    keeps bringing on new warmth
that seems to hold the swallows orbiting
    within their glowing sphere
as I dwell on my own idea of *home.*

    Just one blink and the swallows
momentarily swirl out of sight,
    their circling purple sheen
intensified into a shining thought, and yet
    I speak the swallow syllables
out loud as if the air were listening,
    as if I could respond
by beaming forth a counter-message
    wholly of my own
with *swallow* and its vowel O
    for everyone to hear and feel
when sunlight perches on their arms.
    Although it's true that elsewhere
on this planet earthquake, hurricane,
    eye-socket sealing flood,
and—may we be forgiven—bombs
    assert the baffling rule
of random death and human violence,
    so that I must, as must we all,
seek ways to help, for now,
    this warm and perishable now,
I'll let myself prolong my moment
    in the undiminished sun
as swallows brightly dart out wheeling
    from my shaded eaves,
and I appeal to the transparent air
    for more abundance to unfold
with *home,* a thought-word most mellifluous,
    that leaps forth lightly from my lips
retelling what warm light has told.

2

Person

CONFESSION

    Now that you've asked me to confess—
Though without cause or reason I can see
Unless it is this unrelenting rain—
If after all these years I may have
Hidden something you should know, perhaps
This recollection will surprise you
As recalling it surprises me:

    We spent three days just joking
At the campsite by a lake
That flows into the Allegash in Maine,
Without a nibble, not a bite,
Although my old guide, Will,
Who must have been a logger in Paul Bunyon's days,
Assured me that our luck would change.
    When that third evening came, having tried
Every lure we brought with us,
I went out in a worn canoe with Will,
He steering from the stern,
I scouting from the bow,
Holding a polished rifle on my knees
But with no prey or danger in my mind.
    The sun had set, blue shadows ringed the shore,
And, squinting, in the distant haze I saw
What looked like coasting ducks.
Preceded by a sudden wind,
It seemed as if a storm was on its way,

And yet, despite the rocking of the boat,
I raised my gun for an unlikely shot.
"It's not duck season yet," called Will,
But I had pulled the trigger as he spoke,
And so, as if by miracle, I hit a bird
That flapped up for a second in the air
And then collapsed without a cry.
Astonished by my awful luck,
I wished at once to justify my deed,
And told Will that I wanted to retrieve it
For our evening meal—for sure,
All creatures have to eat to live.
  Returning to our campsite with the duck,
I plucked its clinging feathers off,
Cleaned out the gooey purple organs,
And, because it seemed so scrawny,
Will suggested that I boil it in a pot,
Using his special recipe by adding to the brew
The smoothest, roundest stone
That I could find along the shore.
An eager hour of boiling passed,
And puzzled that no carcass change
Seemed visible, I asked Will when he thought
The duck stew would be done.

  A half a century has gone its way
Since that resounding inquiry,
And I can still see laughter
Glisten in Will's boozy eyes as he replied:
"Be patient, Bob, the damn duck will be done
As soon as that stone melts."

  Shooting that duck can't be my worst sin
If I made a list, and yet somehow
It represents a vague, pervasive guilt

For causing what seems needless harm—
Harm partly driven by intent,
But even more by thoughtlessness.
It's not just the necessity to eat;
I fear that it's not possible to live
According to the choice to do no harm.

   I wonder how much else
I've hidden from you all these years
The fear of doing something really wrong—
A fear that circles me like a blue haze
Half-hidden even from myself,
A trick evasion of some darker thought,
Although in making this confession
As you asked, I doubt that Will could be convinced
Confessed remorse can melt a stone.

THIRST

    First Germany surrendered, then Japan,
Before our senior year at Hengestone High,
And thus the fearless four of us
Could look up at the constellations of the stars
And face what was to come just fortified
With vows that we would stay in touch,
That each of us could count on help, if needed,
From the other three. Al's mother owned a house
Above dunes dense with native roses and tough reeds,
With a vast ocean view
And a guest cabin hidden in the woods
Where we arranged to meet
Before we headed off to college in the fall.
    Ten summers in a row, right after Labor Day,
No matter where we were,
We would reunion there, convinced
We never would forget those years;
Friendship like ours would never change, despite
Bill's claim, "I have a thirst for new experience,"
Which was an annual refrain for him,
A claim more grandiose than his routine
As an aspiring novelist could justify.
We couldn't figure what was troubling him,
Some ailment in his throat perhaps, and yet
One night when Bill had gone to sleep
Before the rest of us, we drove to town
And lassoed a ten-foot plastic Coke bottle

Standing outside a distribution plant,
Hauled it over, pried its bottom open,
And removed the sand that held it in its place.
We tied it to the ski-rack on our jeep,
Absconding with it in the moonlit haze,
And then unloaded it outside the cabin in the woods,
Marked with a sign: DRINK THIS, O THIRSTY ONE!
For Bill to see next morning when he rose.
    That fall Al's cancer-ridden mother died,
Her house was sold, and Al,
Who never had seemed close to her,
Went into mourning for which, so it seemed,
No normal consolation could be found.
After a year, he moved to South Korea, wrote
About a woman he adored who spoke no English,
But I never heard from him again.
And Jack, who of us all, had been the most relieved
To have escaped the draft back then,
Enlisted and became an officer
In the Marines. Soon afterwards,
As if this letter had not been his first,
He wrote to reprimand me I still owed
A debt of service to my country
Still unpaid. I could not bring myself
To answer him; instead, I wrote to Bill,
At work on still another book,
To tell him that reverberating night
We stole the legendary Coke bottle
Under the spectral blur of hazy stars,
To quench his cosmic thirst,
Contained the laughter that I treasured most,
The gold of our sworn friendship and our youth.
      To my astonishment, Bill's curt reply
Was that he had no recollection of his waking up
To find a giant Coke bottle outside

Our cabin in the woods, and wondered
What my motive was for spinning such a tale.
Motive? What motive could I have except
My own ongoing thirst for stars
And laughter reaching out into the night,
Music of friendship we once thought
Eternal as the tides? I'm certain all of this was true,
The breathless theft, the bulletin next morning
On the radio, our restoration of the Coke bottle
Next night despite the first winds of a hurricane.
      Could Bill have chosen to forget all this
Or did he want to claim the story as his own?
And what good could it be to question
What *his* motive was in questioning my motive now,
Since all that's left from the disputed past,
Beyond my late attempt to rescue memory,
Is what was there before we four arrived:
The constellations of the hazy stars,
The ocean view to the horizon's edge,
And, like receding laughter in rough wind,
The tides' undifferentiated slough
Of fractured seashells on the shore?

TWIN POEM

Here is a poem about my fated brother
Who did not get born, a poem about
Our father's death in one swift stroke
And mother's rushed remarriage
To an evasive, melancholy man.

And yet my twin continues in my life
Whenever we converse within a poem
Because—as he once said—having
A sympathetic brother, one like me,
Helps him to realize what kind of man

He might have been despite our father's early death
And mother's sad remarriage to a man
Whose gloom went deeper than a poem
Can reach to cure, whose one defining truth
Was living death through dread of death.

Our father was a man without a twin
To ease his pain, nor could he talk of things
That might distract him from his fear of death—
Sights like the shadow of a solitary man
Strolling along a stony shore,

Whose liquid shade could be my brother
Out enjoying the soft evening air,
Reading a poem about a woman's loneliness.

Walking beside a lake, feeling
Impersonal serenity, as any man

Can feel who steps outside himself, my twin,
Casting his shadow on the lakeside stones
There in the distance with the water birds,
Still shares my history: the truth
Of how a man can reinvent the vanished child

Bred by his parents' suffering.
In the extended sunset of my poem I can
Observe my shadow lengthen on the stones
And leap across the water to a cloud,
Grieved son that once I was, now a grown man.

ARROWHEAD

    Where two streams joined, we met
By accident, sitting upon an outcropping of rock
With only the intent of watching
Water flow beneath unwinding water.
    Facing upstream, she held a flower
To the sun as I leaned back and found
An arrowhead inside a crevice, which lay there
As if someone had left it by intent
As an excuse for me to speak above the whirl of water
Swirling upon stone and thus
Transform the accident of meeting her—
Ablaze in sunlight with a flower in her hand—
Into stark fact as obdurate as rock.
    Could I have called, "Look at this arrowhead
I just found here!" Would she have thought
"An accident, that's credible,"
Or feared that my intent was sinister,
And that the implication of the arrowhead,
Unlike the radiant white flower or
The two streams merging into faster water,
Casting up colored spume,
Had been contrived by me, certain as rock
That forms by geologic laws?
    She had to know an arrowhead
Is humanly designed with the intent to kill,
Though now it's harmless as a flower
Decorating someone's hair,

Or water organized into a fountain
Overflowing with itself.
An arrowhead can now be used
As an adornment for a necklace
Like a flower in a painting where a stream
Leaps past a light-reflecting rock
With nothing in a brushstroke left to accident.
    And so our accidental meeting on the rock
Flowed by, a flower cast upon the water
With intent unknown, and all
That's left now is the arrowhead.

THE FAN'S SOLILOQUY

Were we not put on earth to play,
To strive to win and be the best?
I might have stayed at home all day
And mowed the lawn, been useful, but
I would have missed the game in which
Broad summer is made manifest.
For restless aging fans like me,
Battle's a laughing metaphor,
With tactics of the stolen base,
A covert strategy like war—
The fight to win the pennant race.
The 9th—and all seems lost, but then
We fool them with a bunt—a chance
If missed that will not come again—
To make the eager troops advance
Unless the runner's tagged at home,
The opportunity to score
Is lost, like the lost souls of men,
Now merely shades, for whom no more
Will winning laughter come again.
And so confronted with the fate
Defeat tells us that we deserve
As when a batter hugs the plate,
Misses for the decreed three times
And wonders if that pitcher's curve
Could sneak dawn past a rooster's glare,
A slugger doomed to whiff the air,

Who fails to drive his teammates in
Because the gods are never fair.
And now our team has missed the prize
To bring the pennant flag back home;
They're still heroic in our eyes
Though bonuses will not be much,
According to a contract clause,
Because they failed in the tight clutch.
But so it goes, we fans can see,
According to the iron laws
Revealed as baseball destiny.
Thus they spread out across the land
And merge with all us mortal men,
Aware fate's final score is willed
By forces none can understand
With numbers of a losing sum
That add to no one maimed or killed
Since loss for us is just a game
Unlike the shores of Ilium,
Of Iwo Jima, Normandy,
Where war and play are not the same.

PICNIC

    A picnic table in the forest glade,
Where a stream bends receding in the woods,
Shines so intensely in the morning sun
That no observer can be sure,
Including me, what he thinks may be there
Truly is there: a basket filled
With apples, oranges, and grapes,
And, to the side, inlaid with ivory,
A wooden box—a curiosity for anyone
Who wished to know why she had come,
As if the whole scene were a tapestry.
    The unseen person watching her—
Her hair pulled tightly back,
Her yellow dress a mimic of the sun—
Cannot make waking sense,
With all the fruit, the bread, the cheese,
The full carafe of wine,
Spread on the white, embroidered tablecloth,
Of why she journeyed here alone.
    She seems to glance back
To the path from where she came
That led her to this silent spot—as if
Some reverie of hers were company enough,
Or if this were the place assigned
For opening the box. A man appears
Out from the underbrush
Along the far side of the stream,

Wet to the thighs from crossing there;
And I surmise the watcher can't discern
Exactly who he is: perhaps her father—no,
I'm sure that can't be right
Despite the etched lines by his eyes,
The slight tilt of his lower lip.
He takes her by both hands,
Embraces her until she pulls away.

    The startled watcher makes a sign
That he would interrupt, and yet,
Of course, he's not allowed to interrupt,
That's not the part that watchers play;
How well I know what I can't say to him!
And then another figure enters in
From the far side of that same stream.
He too is wet, his wilder hair
Aslant across one eye, and the observer thinks
That he might be the first man's son.

    The watcher feels relief,
And so, to my surprise, do I
Just as a sudden wind excites the leaves,
When her white arms embrace and hold
The younger man, her fingers spread
Around his ears, her eyes squeezed shut
So that she doesn't see the older man
Retreat into the shade beyond the scene.

    But this is wrong—the watcher's got it wrong:
The younger man is not the elder's son,
Who as all stories go must win the girl;
He is the youth the older man once was.
The older man must lose her
To his former self, surely as if
She had been guarded by a unicorn.

    And yet the watcher isn't certain
There's a difference in their faces or their arms,

Their sleeves rolled up to show their strength,
For all the watcher sees
From his place in concealing shade
Is that a younger man drives out an older
Empty-handed back into the woods.
    The scene is misted in an umber haze
So that I cannot ease
The watcher of his vexed uncertainty
Or ease the darkening
Of my own earlier relief:
Of those two men, whom does he think he is?
In the eternal story of himself,
How old is he? He is not able to decide
If that young woman guarded in the glade
Can understand exactly whom she chose
To send away or whom to keep,
Though like the blank expanse of open sky,
The baffled watcher feels bereft,
And I allow myself to share
His longing for a story that can satisfy.
    Although I'll never know
(Or maybe I forgot) what she kept hidden
In her inlaid box or why she had to bring it
To this sunlit circle in the woods—
Perhaps dark rubies that her mother left
As an inheritance—I still can almost taste
The tang of fruit upon my lips and tongue,
The spongy bread, the pungency of wine;
I still can hear the rumbling water
Where the roused stream bends,
And see that staunch observer
Standing transfixed in the woven shade.

MIDSUMMER MUSIC

Plump summer pauses here, an opera
To express exuberance: a duet
In the ascending spirit of *amor*,
Between warm wind and wafted trees, an aria,
Glissando, from a stream,
Then whirring hummingbirds, and then a hint of silence
That portends *addio*
In a raven's shadow over stone,

Smooth as an oboe's run. The stone
Is central since an opera—
The form itself an aspect of *amor*—
Requires symbolic scenery for the duet
Of separating lovers whose soft stream
Of mingled notes holds back more silence
Time's own unintentional *addio*
Will restore. But now a father's aria

Storms out his grief, responding to the aria
His daughter sang that turned to stone
The down-pour of his heart, moaning *addio*—
According to the laws of opera—
On learning she is caught up in a stream
Of passion for his rival's son, which a duet,
Returning to the main theme of *amor*,
Will later clarify, since nothing's left to silence

Till the story ends, though that's a silence,
My dear listener, beyond the cure of opera,
Beyond the choiring of *addio*.
But now summer sun sings its blithe aria
Of light and air, and the inquiring stream
Plucks pebbles *pizzicato* on the stone
In syncopation with the mind's duet
Of sight and scenery, *amor*

Uniting nature with rejoining art, *amor*,
The harmony in which each stone
Extends itself by echoing the stream.
Her father's rival is aroused whose aria,
Basely aspiring to the throne, booms out *addio*
To remorse, concealing jealous silence
Not to be relieved in duel or duet,
So he can't be redeemed within the opera.

And yet we all love evil in an opera—
Maladizione! ah, the word is its own aria,
Like August thunder crashing upon stone
As if the stone's own silence
Spoke in deep crescendos of *addio*
Which in turn inspire a new duet,
A rainbow with its choral message of *amor*
That arcs through mountain mist down to the stream,

Revealing to the lovers this same stream
Is where they first sang their farewell. And now *amor*,
Despite her father's curse—possessive silence
Seething underneath his aria—
Again is given voice, transforming his *addio*
Into balm for hope, transfiguring the stone
Into a symbol of the strength of opera,
So that the lovers' consummate duet,

In marriage or in death, is a duet
Resolving family discord as past silence
Is forsworn, although no opera,
Dear listener, keeps time forever, no *amor*
Outlives its signifying stone,
And no incantatory stream,
In all the flowing sweetness of its aria,
Outsings time's mindless ultimate *addio,*

Which reminds us that our opera's *addio,*
Every chorus, each duet, each aria,
Is no more than a stream's *allegro* over stone
Or silence as a rest-note for *amor.*

CLONE

　　Someone's got to be first, so why not me—
I'm just as worthy of achieving immortality
As any of you, so I'll make my move
Whether or not the multitude approve,
Before old-fashioned time runs out,
Now with red apple buds wafting about
My whirling head; and now I wave my hat
To welcome swallows to their habitat.
　　My qualms, I'm sure, are habits from a past
Now obsolete, old forms that need not last,
But should I call him brother or my son,
And since clandestine doubts have now begun
To sway my mind, should I define myself to be
His mother or his dad when he
Requires my comfort in the quaking night
Or takes his self-delight from my delight?
Worse still, should I consider him
Another version of myself, steadfast and grim,
Muscled like me, guarding his place,
A half-defiant grin fixed on his face?
　　And here's what vexes me the most:
Would I be loving him or just a ghost
Of who I am or was? And if my life alone
Does not suffice in my own flesh and bone,
Would not a rhyming replica of me
Increase this very insufficiency?
Concerns our species never faced before

Burden my thoughts and roar
Like winds that crack the tops of trees,
So I had better pause to feel the ease
Of this still soothing evening light,
To take time out to contemplate the sight
Of swallows swooping to their nest
Beneath my eaves, a necessary rest
From agitated thought that doubles back
And sets me coupling with myself upon a rack.
    A final hesitation might yet quell the greed
That gnaws in me, that most fantastic need
To be both parents packaged in one pod—
(A wish, I do suspect, to be like God).
Still, taking time does not negate time, it's a pause,
Not an escape; both end and cause
At once, time thus feels tender as the flowing air
With breeding swallows circling everywhere.
    But what if my son-clone resents me still
As children must, determined by the will
To break free from the binding past,
And how could he break free at last,
Seize his own time, if in his blood he's caught
In chains of what my set of genes has wrought?
And would he then wish also to rebel
From one law through time immemorial
Requiring parents, in blind faithfulness,
To set life forth to curse or bless,
Not knowing what their blend would bring
To darkness or to light? While honoring
Uncertainty, they'd send a child out on his way
As leaves uplifted by a wind still play
Autumnal tunes of timeliness, and then let go,
Aware no swallows fill a time of snow.
    But I have virtues to perpetuate,
Hatred of all the hatefulness I hate;

I treasure swirling rivers and lush trees,
Bluster of roses and the boom of bees;
My heart goes out to suffering;
I sing a song the disappointed sing;
Surely a clone of mine, as nature's aid,
Would help replenish love. The world is made
To be remade; remaking's good if through him I
Can override my dark wish not to die.
    But no, afraid of time, I'm still time's fool,
Seeking to change the one unchanging rule
That all must change, that I must set him free
From my vain wish to parent my paternity—
A wish which grimaces at me, its clone,
Locked in for all eternity alone.

BETRAYAL

    The blunt need to betray
Quickens Jack's calculating heart
When entering the house where his best friend
Was unaware his own wife was his enemy,
The wife he'd have to struggle to forgive
For their kids' sakes—if he
Proved capable of reasoning.
    And as Jack climbs up to her room—
His friend so trustingly away—
Jack's passion now to test
How much she can forgive
Roils in his thickened heart,
Though one can hardly call this reasoning,
This torment to betray
As if unfaithfulness could somehow free
Her passion to forgive his tempting her.
    But why should she forgive
Either herself or him, her lover-enemy,
Whose heart lurks in the traffic of the street,
Awaiting chance to summon him?
    As if greed was grim nature's reasoning,
Its law inscribed on his stone heart—
To injure so that others can forgive—
Jack's body now becomes his forsworn enemy:
He sees her smoky eyes reveal
That she will not forgive him,
That he should have stayed true as her friend.

    Descending to the neon street
Among the traffic's movement to no end,
Blinking its constancy of friendless red,
Jack mingles facelessly
With all the unforgiven who cannot forgive,
The faithless living, and the faithful dead.

DIVORCE

"I'm sure they did the best they could,"
She tells herself, and she can still recall
The day they sat her down in her own room,
Her mother clutching her pet elephant,
Not touching one another, looking
Only at her. "Why can't you try again?" was all
She thought to say. They were a window's width
Apart, and she could see across the field,
Down to the lake, and now it seemed
The calm geese floated in a ring
Whenever she looked back to fix the day
Her childhood ended and the self
She would become fastened its grip.
The woman whom he left her mother for—
What power did she have, since she was not
That beautiful? And was it for her sake,
As once it slipped out from her mother's lips,
That she had turned down other men?
Now when her mother came to visit her,
They'd talk about her mother's loneliness,
So who was taking care of whom, and what
Explained why she could never trust herself
To trust somebody else—as if
Failure were written in the stars?
Statistics showed that children of divorce
Were also likely to divorce, so maybe
This defeat of hers was not her fault—

And, to be honest, it felt right to blame
Her mother or her father still depending
On whose story she believed—so how
Could she not feel a little pity for herself?
The story of her life ached in her heart,
And who, now that she lived alone,
Was left to share her heartache with?
She closes her tired eyes and once again
She sees the stately geese float back and forth
Across the shadow of the willow tree
She used to climb against her parents' rules.
And now a shocking thought occurs to her:
What if the pain she feels is not
In some deep sense her own; what if it is
Something impersonal, something she shares
With everyone, some double consciousness
Reflecting what all human creatures undergo
No matter what their circumstance?
Awareness that we are aware
Of longing for some permanence that cannot be;
She's sure that is the cause, human
And inescapable, and yet if only she could have
Another chance at happiness—
Her parents reuniting, she trusting in herself,
And light upon lake water undulating
In its stationary place, the geese
Still circling silently as if just watching them
Were all that thought required of her
And nothing needed to be understood.

JOURNEY

"No, no, I can't explain my restlessness;
Don't think of it as my response to you!
But there's a joke, my dear, about a quest

Made by a man like me, named Dan, who knew
One thing about himself: he had to find
Life's meaning, so he sailed to Katmandu

To interview a famous sage, old, blind,
Attired in rags, who claimed in a hushed voice,
"Life is a fountain." Astonished by that kind

Of statement, Dan complained, "There's nothing worse
Than proclamations that mean anything;'
The sage glared red as if to lay a curse,

But what surprisingly came out could bring
Someone to laughing tears: "You mean life's not
A fountain?" sage replied. "This joke might ring

Your funny bells if it's stretched further out,"
Dan tells his wife, but she suspects that he
Is hiding something he can't talk about,

And so, dear readers, with due modesty,
I'll share Dan's tale of secrecy and strife
And we shall see whatever we shall see.

Observe him, then, just midway in his life,
A journeyer at heart, if metaphor
Contains its own slant truth. A wary wife

To query him, grown sons whom he adores,
Daughters to add mixed sweetness to his days,
Fair friends and unfair enemies galore,

Provide him with a multitude of ways
To keep himself distracted. But a quest
Now beckons him; I hope that it's O.K.

With you who still attend me here since *quest*'s
A philosophic term, and yet it's true,
So I'll go with the flow and make the best

Of what words spring to mind, and if I do,
Dante will find a place in paradise
For me to spin my tale, maybe to you

If readers' virtues bring you to those skies.
Let's kindly scrutinize how Dan will test
Himself when challenged, his bold enterprise

Of thinking—self-protected with a jest,
Of course—thoughts that acknowledge his new need
For self-awareness. The unsettled rest

Of his remaining life begins in greed
For some redeeming revelation, some
Consuming sense that what ripe life can breed

Is more than just more breeding life to come
But with no goal in sight except for genes
To replicate themselves, the sum

Of their fecundity the groping means
Not one jot different than their groping end.
The sky now darkens over Dan—it seems

The sun is covered by the moon to send
An omen as in Shakespeare's plays: his life
Must change, whatever fate that might portend.

He shudders to explain this to his wife:
What would she make of it? He tells his boss:
"Work's daily satisfactions don't suffice

As happiness"; his daughters, at a loss
For words provide hugs that his need requires;
His sons, perversely unimpressed, are cross

In their abrupt response. But he's on fire
With new conviction blazing in his heart,
And now he forges action from desire,

And he sets sail. For an auspicious start
He needs to contemplate the wine-dark sea
Since roiling water's always played a part

Expressing something fundamental we
Can find in nature, some profound design—
Permanence of ephemerality.

And yet his journeying demands he find
Some moral purpose that's more personal
Than ceaseless, everlasting flux, unkind

Ongoing processes to which we all
At last succumb. And so his ship heads where
The mists of China swirl up in the fall.

But three days out, enraptured as he stares
At the illuminated spume and spray,
In disengagement from himself—his prayer

Already answered in the dreamy way
His mind detaches from itself—the ship
Shifts sideways and he falls into the sway

Of starlit waters, while upon his lips
The taste of salt usurps his garbled cry
As he sinks deeper and his fingertips

Slowly reach toward the warped arch of the sky.
With awesome wonder overtaking fear,
What flashes back, without his knowing why,

Curled in her hibernating den, a bear,
Ready to reemerge into new woods,
Snorts softly as her hot gaze holds him there.

Then everything goes whirling dark; his blood
Can't squeeze another breath, but in a rush
As if the sea bursts from its darker mood,

A sperm whale surges under him to push
Him back to the ship's deck. Yes, breath is good,
And, his mind clearing, he recalls the hush

Of facing death when hiking through dense woods,
Confronted by a bear, he and his wife
Clung to each other with a grip that could

Outlast its cause by adding life to life
By what thoughts of the loss of life inspire.
So what, then, was Dan searching for, what strife

Had now become fresh power to aspire?
When he arrives in China as dawn air
Swells in his lungs and quickens his desire,

A cloud-ringed mountain beckons him to dare
The rocky, three-day perilous ascent
To find the Buddhist monk residing there

Beyond love's disenchantments. Since Dan's spent
His hoarded capital on the belief
This monk might offer clues to what Life meant

In authoring the history of grief
As if pain served some cause, he makes the climb,
Assisted by a guide, and great relief

Sweeps over him, though he has crossed the line
Into white flowing realms, when he discerns
Smoke curling from a cave—as if Dame Time,

Mist mingled with the whirling snow, returns
Before his startled eyes. A face appears
From the dank recess of the cave and spurns

His brash advance with a demeaning sneer
Informing him that he will have to wait
The mythic usual three days, like years,

Before the monk will talk to him. "That's fate,"
Dan tells himself with new serenity,
And though blunt wind flares up, not one blast late,

The monk emerges, dropping to his knees
And in a mesmerizing flutelike voice,
Suggesting rather that he is a she,

Seems safely beyond suffering and choice.
Half understood by her interpreter,
Dan's steady guide, she penetrates the noise

Of swirling winds and knows—she doesn't err—
What he has come to learn: Life's meaning, nothing less.
And so Dan's question does not startle her,

Although there's no room now for one to guess
Whether "Life is a fountain!" is her claim,
Since you've all heard this joke before, and, yes,

I'm sure you also can recall what she exclaimed,
Responding to Dan's disappointed look,
"You mean life's not a fountain?" Ah! Dan aims

A wink at her according to the book
My version of his story's free to improvise
To keep you trusting readers on the hook.

And now, newly inspired, Dan gamely tries
To spur the monk to think of something new
Beyond the human heart's banalities.

"It all depends on your criteria for *true*,"
She croons, "so say I'm young and beautiful
When you return; inform your wife that you

Fell faithlessly in love with me." A swell
Of pathos rises in Dan's heart although
He fears what his surmise of her reveals

About himself, and knows he cannot know
If she discloses what she truly feels
By turning pain to comedy, which grows

To cosmic laughter that includes us all.
And maybe in some wishful sense (for who
Lives free of fantasy?) we're beautiful

And young in rhyme, and maybe when we woo
The universe with metaphor and say
"Life is a fountain," what we really do

Is tell ourselves that truth lies in the way
That words, evasive and elliptical,
Are laughing words that flow in flowing play.

And now Dan's laughing at himself—a full,
Galactic laugh that echoes up beyond
The mountain crags; no longer in control,

She's laughing with him in a misty bond
That joins them to the windy elements.
And so he sails back home in high command

Of the vague spirits whom he always meant
To conjure from the sea's ancestral life—
Vexed spirits of still undisclosed intent.

When safely back on shore, Dan tells his wife:
"You seem more youthful now, more beautiful;
Our life together surely is enough;

Renewed choice makes our marriage bountiful."
Later when Dan's wife questioned me: "I see
Defiant laughter in him that can heal

All wounds; I know Dan just as I know me,"
Was my assurance that he hadn't lied.
She asked if that was *my* epiphany.

"Life is . . . Life *is* a fountain," I replied.

RETURNING

    I do not long for paradise
Beyond my misted mountain home,
But then I've not been driven out
Like those poor souls from Kosovo,
All their belongings lost,
And how can they decide
To risk returning with life so unsure?
    Secluded by surrounding trees,
I don't know what to wish for them—the lost,
Driven from smoking Kosovo—
(Would just return for them be paradise?)
And thus I can't decide,
Late though it is,
How I can make myself at home
Amid the rubble of my mind
And not get lost
In thoughts so troubled and unsure
That earthly paradise
Beneath my hawk-spun mountain peaks
Becomes a Kosovo.
    Knowing that I don't know
Leaves me unsure, even
When I decide to spend my empathy
On those with their lost dead,
Imagining they're with me now
Among the quaking aspen leaves.

    Yes, I can make myself at home
Right here on earth if I decide
That being lost only means being lost
Within my mind, dreaming
Of emptied Kosovo
Where slit throats of the lost
Are like fine fissures in the rock.
    Unsure for one split second
If they've died at home,
Nothing remains for them then to decide,
While safe among dense evergreens,
I wonder how I can
Bear witness to cleansed Kosovo
And still not have to pay
The price of paradise.

THE BOOK

    A muffled snap,
A puff of exhaled breath,
And then it's closed within the hum
That seals its sudden silence in,
Silence encircling itself
Until there's nothing left to listen for,
Nothing to anticipate.

    How long that nothing lasts—
A minute, a millennium, or more,
How can one know, since knowing has
Its own small humming sound, like
Trilling water running over stones,
The sipping sounds that deer lips make—
As if awareness in the universe
Might start, or start again, from nothing more
Than such suggestive sibilants,
The hint of such astounding words to come,
Of words abounding everywhere.

    Then here he is, and she with him,
A snake entwined within smooth branches and
Fruit ruddy wondrous to behold.
And therein doth a story start
Of disobedience and blame,
Of brothers at their fateful odds,
A father's would-be sacrifice,

Inscrutable to everyone except his God,
And everywhere unburied skulls,
Washed clean by genocidal waters
Gleaming in the midday sun
With jaws agape, as if about to speak
To tell their version of the story
That's unfolding once again. A book
Has been reopened and its characters
Are doomed or privileged
To live their lives again,
Survival-longing in their bones,
Making whatever peace they can
With words they glean from warning fire
In a bush, from angry thunder,
Or a whirlwind of chastising air.

  Out of the silence underneath the stream
Beneath the tree, out of mere nothingness,
A voice now summons me to find myself
In a succession of interpreters:
"Speak to the young," it says,
"Tell them to listen, listen hard,
Tell them about the dreadful book you love."

TWO JEWS ON A TRAIN

I trace this story back a hundred years
    before the holocaust
to a quaint town in Poland where each house
    had its own chimney of red bricks.
That's where my great-great-uncle Jacob lived
    (I still can't figure out precisely
just how many greats is right), a prosperous
    shoemaker with a loyal wife,
twelve children in full health, and each twelve
    with twelve more to call their own—
almost enough to make a nation of his family.
    Jacob awoke one morning
with a nameless weight pressing his heart,
    although the sunlit air
above the vendor-teeming streets seemed
    filled with glowing wings.
I should have said eleven children
    flourished in his eyes,
because the twelfth, his youngest girl,
    (sometimes I need a second try
to get things accurate) could not
    find for herself a proper mate
to love her, and whom she in turn could love.
    She seemed fated to suffer
and endure just for being who she was.
    Jacob decided he would seek advice

in Krakow from the famous rabbi, Gluckenluft,
    interpreter of holy texts.
He put on his best suit (in truth his only one)
    and bought a first-class ticket
on the early train. Chance had determined
    that he should be seated by
a fellow townsman, a skilled carpenter,
    who suffered heartache
very like his own because his third son,
    born with a red blotch upon his cheek,
could not keep the good job he counted on.
    The carpenter, his rough hands
folded on his lap, also was journeying to Krakow
    to consult the esteemed Gluckenluft.
Jacob and Joseph shared the same grim sense
    of unimaginable misfortune
pending throughout the heedless universe,
    (and yet what sorrow
can be truly new? they thought) and talked nonstop,
    and laughed despite themselves,
as if their conversation could forestall
    the next calamity they prophesied
was sure to come. They knew the precedents,
    established at the start, as when the Lord
warned Abraham of years of wandering,
    (400 years to be exact) before
his promised seed would be allowed to settle
    in a land that they could call their own.
Perhaps their stubborn gloom somehow
    was merited; perhaps
there lurked in them some hidden guilt
    still unacknowledged and still
unconfessed, some failure to be thankful
    for the daily blessings

of just ordinary things: fresh bread or ripened fruit
    or wild contagious laughter
as the children whirled and scurried
    to prepare themselves for school.
Even the sight they now enjoyed
    out from the window of the train
where fields of harvest wheat, though streaming by,
    seemed somehow permanent,
illuminated by mild morning sun,
    cried out for gratitude.
When finally they got to smoky Krakow
    and were graciously admitted
to the book-lined study where the rabbi prayed,
    they each recounted what had seemed
the undeserved and spiteful sorrows
    laid upon their children's lives—
although sufficiently content
    with what their own lives offered them—
and asked for wisdom how parental grief
    might gracefully be borne.
The rabbi paused. He'd had a dream, he said,
    the very night before
they had appeared at his own door—a dream
    in which the Lord enlightened him:
it never was His plan to shape a world
    where easy solace could be found,
except perhaps for brief forgetfulness
    while making love
or watching birds migrating in the fall;
    only that life be interesting
was what He intended from the start.
    "I want the story of the world
to be worth passing on," the rabbi quoted Him
    as if possessed and in a trance.

Upon returning home, this version
    of the Lord's revealed intent
was what excited Jacob told his wife,
    although she died it seemed
without a cause soon afterward,
    one thunderous and windy evening
in her kitchen baking bread as lightning flared
    the jagged edges of the clouds.
(So who knows what it might have meant to her—
    those thoughts the Lord supposedly
revealed?) And Jacob's unloved daughter,
    although doubly loved by him,
never got married; yet the diary she kept,
    bound in the softest leather
that she could afford—and which I hold
    uncertain in my hands—admits
she had suspected that her father
    made the story up as something
he could leave behind to please her
    when his little puff of life was gone.

EVENING MEDITATION

Isaac sat on the swing
on his slaked wooden porch
looking out past a field
    where fat sheep grazed.
The tilled field ended
    with a twisted fence
beyond which old oaks intertwined
so that slant western light
    barely shone through.
He heard a wail unwind
from the obscuring trees,
    assuming it must be
some preyed-on animal.

The porch's overhang
sheltered vexed Isaac from
    the sleeting rain and wind,
from humid summer heat
of that late breezeless hour,
but could not shelter him
    from his own thoughts
because one can't think not to think
or choose to block out memory,
but more because what burdened him,
    I must assume,

was inescapable uncertainty—
    like weather in his mind—
for nothing that he could define.

His memory surged back
to when he told a joke about
    a crippled man,
cuckolded by his wife,
forgetting that there was
a short, clubfooted man there in the room,
and he was overwhelmed
by his incredible stupidity
    when tidal silence
rippled through the audience.

How many times had he seen
needless pain inflicted by
    somebody unaware,
without intention to cause hurt?
We just don't ever know enough,
    or have sufficient time
to think enough, Isaac
commiserated to himself,
or maybe some occurrences,
    Isaac half wished,
are best not understood
or best just left to accident.

Perhaps the vague remorse—
    if that was what he felt—
was larger, more impersonal:
the failure to alleviate
    a stranger's suffering

or take that starved cat in
    who's rubbing bleakly
up against the window pane?

Yet was such suffering
    inseparable from
some deep, inscrutable design
like that cry from the woods
or his unwilled stupidity?
    Why blame himself,
he surely must have thought,
for what has always been
    unchangeable—
like causing unintended pain,
like wishing not to think
    the thoughts one thinks?

And Isaac's memory flew back
to when he was a boy before
    the soldiers came,
to when his father took
the silver candelabrum
    that his grandfather
had polished every year
to celebrate the feast of lights,
    and, for protection,
buried it within the woods.

He knows he cannot know
    himself, and Isaac
could not figure out, although
    he must have tried,
whether his dark-eyed father
dug the candelabrum out
after the shouting soldiers left,

nor could he find a reason why
    his father might
have left it there to merge
with other fossils of defeat,
    as if it were a sacrifice
to the unknown, without
    an explanation
that could ease a young man's mind.

EVASION

for Larry Raab

I wait here for my other self, my life,
To join me where, let's say, I'm sitting
On a promontory looking out
Across the wild and wind-swept sea,
The wave crests almost regular
Like those ribbed overhanging clouds.
Wild roses, gnarled and blighted by some bug,
Make up the backdrop of my vantage point,
Though I am focused on the sea,
Watching my mind attend upon itself,
Watching my youthful mother nursing
My new sister in smooth summer shade
As now—seven decades on—my sister
Tucks our deaf-blind mother into bed
And feeds her pills to ease her into sleep
That she both dreads and craves.
What can connect my sense of me
From where my life has been
To where I'm sitting now
Among wild roses staring at the waves
As they come cresting in again?
Who was that person digging in moist April earth
To plant a maple or a birch,
Or should I choose the bending figure
Of a snowy January night
As my right representative, lost
In a book about how stars were formed

Or how the laws for organizing words
Got scripted in the neurons and the synapses
Of the evolving human brain?
Yet everywhere I turn I meet a self
That turns away, evades
My grimly scrutinizing gaze,
As if reluctant to be known,
A self that seems to realize itself
Within a scene composed of its own vanishing
With everything and everybody gone.
Each star, each tree, each rose, each book,
Even the spume-spray of the ocean
Underneath its ghostly clouds
Are thoughts that thin out like
The spreading silence of the universe—
Thin out so lightly everywhere
That I no longer separate myself
From the white calm of the surrounding air.

3

Perspective

WHAT WOULD WIND SAY?

Gathering grief has settled in my eyes,
    my body loses its solidity.
The lost past, like dense shade, drifts further still;
    where are my hours and days, where are they now?
Now soon enough I'll be with you, unrecognized;
    I'll wander down the dust
    without the ease of wandering.
What good to have a life set down in words?
    I pause at the sharp edge of what is sayable;
my friends reach out, but I'm not there;
    my enemies find me invisible.
I'm just an oboe played beneath a tree,
    a flute-note faint beyond a stream.
If I could find assertion in complaint,
    who'd listen; if I uttered out a curse,
    who would take heed?
Can reason talk one out of one's despair;
    can consolation be called forth
    and made obedient?
I'm glad the circling eagle has no use for me;
    the raven's raucous cry comes close enough;
the deer are curious, but not for long;
    the bear cubs keep the mother bear in sight;
    I'm brother to the bobcat and the owl.
Is it not totally astonishing
    that I take notice of myself? For what?
What would wild wind or rising water say

>were they, too, burdened
>with vain consciousness?
>
>I make do with my making do,
>>and for a moment I forget myself,
>
>but then awareness, summoned not by me,
>>returns of its own brute accord;
>
>one thought of you—and you are gone again.
>>Again you vanish, and now still again
>
>what is not there—is there as palpable
>>as stone with etched-in words
>
>for some pale stranger passing by.
>>Your absence is as bright
>>as sunlight on the sea,
>
>illuminating the receding depths of air,
>>blue fading into softer blue as if
>
>some random thought of fading blue
>>extended everywhere.

DISTANCE

Deciduous, yes that's a soothing word;
It feels smooth like a maple leaf
And shares with sharper evergreens,
Whose needles even to the sight are rough,

A sheen that carries through the forest haze
Yet brings you near, as if you spoke the sound,
Deciduous, from a lost past now so remote,
That smooth is no less sorrowful than rough.

Pine evergreen, and hemlock evergreen,
So distant yet so near, still sooth my heart
And smooth the passageway through rough terrain
That keeps my shadow whispering, *deciduous,*

Far from our first embrace where oaks
Are evergreen in memory,
Receding deep into the forest haze
Where still my unsoothed heart makes its abode.

So I'll take all the soothing
Of deciduous renewal I can get,
For there's not shade enough to smooth
The lingering of kisses lost,

The rough road of relinquishing
That leads into the heart's own haze

Where blurring shadows merge,
Making ongoing sorrow smooth

And all loss so breathtaking near
Love cannot tell if loss is smooth or rough,
Deciduous or evergreen,
As far away as when we met, or here.

FAINT MEMORY

    Lugubriously played, a Chopin nocturne
Floats across the sleek unruffled lake
From the pale lantern-lit pavilion
On the exclusive other side,
To where we stand beneath a willow tree
With me about to kiss you if
Unsteady nerves do not betray desire.
    How, I now wonder, did soft orange lights
Upon reflecting water, mingled
With sharp points of quickened stars,
Express what I then felt—your image
Lurking somewhere in my mind—and yet
Projected on an outer world?
    Or maybe something other outside me
Had fixed that moment in my mind
And made itself interior,
Had burned anticipation of a kiss
Upon what would become my memory
So that the wide and windless night
From over half a century ago,
With us beneath a weeping willow tree,
Is consummation I desire still,
Though its not happening has faded
Even as actual kisses do.
    I hear it still, music that seemed then
Rising from the lake, its melodies
Somehow embodied in reflected light,

And your white face uncannily familiar
Underneath the moonlit shadows of dense leaves,
As if I'd known you from another life.
    And is what I feel now also familiar
Or entirely new: extended silence
Following the last note in diminished air,
The certainty of knowing I can't know,
Desire reluctant to fulfill desire,
Like water in itself without a form,
Without another place to go?

CONTENTMENT

This is the day I've waited for;
    The lion lies down with the lamb;
    And everything I was and am
Is ripe without desire for more.

Cruel eating ceases on this day;
    There is no hiding and no chase;
    Sufficient is the time and place
To be as if to be were play.

All lovers make a rightful pair;
    The child feels thanks with nothing owed
    For what the parents have bestowed.
A harvest blessing fills the air:

A breeze that first gave Adam breath
    When life was one with gratitude—
    A heartfelt thought, a worded mood
That had no argument with death.

The stream I chill to walk across
    Preserves each pebble in its voice;
    Its song has no idea of choice
Or change, and so it can't know loss.

It doesn't know it doesn't know
    And can't tell was from yet to come

  Or even where it started from;
There's only flow, there's only flow.

I've nothing further to discover;
  I shudder that I've dreamed it all—
  What follows after gaudy fall
When this awaited day is over.

MOLECULAR CELEBRATION

for Bill Bevis

    Hardly a single cell that thrived
In my brave body seven years ago,
Not blood, not gut, not flesh,
Not even bone, remains alive today,
And yet, surprisingly, I'm me, still me,
Still who I was.
    Despite this transformation,
Something has stayed the same
Through some device of consciousness:
I know that I continue to be Bobby Pack
Who once upon a long lifetime ago
Played stoopball in the Bronx
And won more often than I lost—although
A kid (I think his name was Stanley)
Might dispute this fact. But even if he's right,
That would not alter who I was or am.
    Perhaps I can compare myself
To that sea-worthy wooden boat
Its captain loved so well: each day
He'd have another plank replaced
Until no single board remained
From when the boat was built, and yet
It looked, and seemed, (and was?) the same,
With its original identity;
And just as every breath of air
The captain breathed contained some molecules
All other journeyers inhaled,

Back even to Cro-Magnon times,
Does that make him (and me!) a carbon copy
In some binding sense of every
Strutting one of us who ride the earth?
    Dear sharers of my molecules,
Brothers and sisters in the bond of hydrogen,
Allow the glisten of the foaming boat
To serve as the defining emblem of
My wayward consciousness
Aware of its own self, including
Random thoughts that merely pop
Into a momentary focus in my mind:
My mountain-climbing daughter dangling
From a rope; the ravished bear who stole
The suet I had left out for the woodpeckers;
The apple trees I planted just last spring
Whose buds are still too tight to tell
If they survived April's late freeze.
                            And now—
The very now in which I write these words—
Mozart's G-minor string quintet
Moves to the forefront of my mind,
Which has been playing on my stereo
And seems projected back to fill
The spaces of the reinvented past, the scene
When Stan and I competed sweating
In the steaming Bronx. (I won!)
    The inescapable deep need
Wells up in me to make some order
Of these memories, which I allowed
To flow forth without sense of where they'd lead—
The way the universe, without a goal,
Just by expanding, has put forth
Its galaxies, its stars, a solar system,
And a single planet with an atmosphere

That could breed thoughtful life to come.
    But no, my mind feels quite at home
In its perversity today, even
Relieved, enlightened, so I won't insist
On a definitive conclusion—like
A plunging boat returned to harbor—
For this disquisition on identity.
    I'll just recline and contemplate
How cells, like people, come and go,
Uncelebrated and unmourned,
Until their structure (me!) breaks down
Into its basic chemistry, which once
Was mostly water anyway,
and nothing's left to wonder or to care
But background cosmic radiation
From our distant origin, like notes
Of Mozart's music spreading everywhere.

THE CEILING

In fifty years . . . we're likely to discover which aspects of biology are irreducibly complex . . . We will be limited by complexity ceilings.

—Jaron Lanier

But can I make my older self at home
In such a vaulted house where I would find
Floors laid with aching body facts I know,
The ceiling my awareness of my mind
Much too complex to know itself—a house
With windows searching past contending trees
To where rough barren mountain peaks repose
In snow-swirled mist; or maybe to the sea
Past flotsam desolate upon the shore?
Can I reside in sights mind comprehends,
Things just themselves that memory can store,
Though vexed by questionings of cloudy ends,
And cherish self-eluding life while, yes,
Relinquishing the wish for happiness?

GO JUMP

By Darwinian standards I am a horrible mistake . . . But I am happy to be voluntarily childless, ignoring the solemn imperative to spread my genes. And if my genes don't like it, they can go jump in the lake.

—*How the Mind Works*, Steven Pinker

Inspired by your "mistake," I'll order mine
To do the same. So, Steven, watch them race
Like kids along a dock, grab their rough knees,
Plunge in ass first. June heat provides this place

(Approved with my deliberate assent)
Beside a willow tree, for them to take
A holiday from replication's work,
Disturbing their reflections in the lake.

And thus I liberate myself to will
The self-willed life high thought aspires to live
While they are splashing in wild play,
Released from the solemn imperative

That kept me hot in sexual pursuits,
A robot driven proud by jealousy.
And while they frolic in fresh merriment,
I choose autonomous philosophy,

Unburdened of Darwinian desires,
And make peace with base instincts that have led
Me to the edge, emboldened by your book
That claims my mind has power to slay the dread

Old dragon of grim evolution's laws.
So when my genes return from their long swim,
Have dried their little backsides in the sun—
Fathered from leaping laughter at your whim—

What voluntary metaphor can you
In happiness paternally provide
To send them packing home inside my blood
Where lust and mirthless vanity reside?

MARVELING

(About a Possibly Not So Coy Mistress)

     Well, Andrew, there's a lot that we know now
You didn't know, so if, though me, you woo
Again, figure that she's familiar with
That *carpe diem* pitch (translated by
A recent wit as the "catch of the day")
In which your talk of worms raised that grave theme—
The fleetingness of unappeasing time—
Most promising in your persuading her.
     You'll have to be less fancy in the way
You flirt in this new age: worship is out,
So is salacious praise of body parts.
She knows that male resource investment, our
Expenditure of semen, if compared
To her nutritious egg, is equal to
The eating of just one potato chip,
And that a fertilizing sperm—of all
The billions easily available
Whose strategy suggests we play the field—
Is only DNA with a long tail
To steer it wombward from the nether end.
     But here's the breakthrough concept that you must
Keep fixed in mind: a huge advantage lies
In self-deception if compliance is
Your heart's true goal: if you do not yourself
Believe you love her, she'll detect your lie,
Or even your minute uncertainty;
Yes, evolution has bestowed on her

The gift of seeing through poetic talk
Of "wingéd chariots" and "birds of prey,"
Since making a poor choice of someone who
Won't stick around to help support the kids
Lowers her prospect for successful genes,
Her one real claim to immortality.
    Yet knowing that one must deceive oneself
To be persuasively sincere, how does
A guy deliberately fall in love
And pledge, with a committed heart, his sperm-self
Will be faithful for eternity?
Andrew, that's tough, not even science can
Resolve that paradox, so let's return
To what continues to seem genuine
When urged by you in your own time—the worms
As dark devourers of virginity.
That suspect tactic still seems pretty gross—
Evoking bodily disgust is not
Ideal for quickening desire—and yet
It carries a sure sense of urgency,
Which she can't view as hypocritical.
    But if we want to be more balanced in
Our view of worms—they're not just metaphors—
Let's express gratitude to their moist kind
For helping to improve old clotted soil
So plants can grow, and, while we're at it, let's
Offer our praise to all bacteria,
Without whose efforts nothing would decay.
The long perspective says decay is good;
Without it, bones would haunt us everywhere,
And that's as gross as gruesome thought can get.
    Aha! My point about how easily
We can distract ourselves by citing facts
We know indeed are true (billions of hopeful sperm
Are easily produced upon a dreamy afternoon)

Is demonstrated here. Let's count on it;
Let's put our faith in our ability
To turn deception into its own truth,
For, after all, in punning how you can't
Stop time and make the sun (spelled S-U-N)
Stand still, yet you can make HIM run (if spelled
That would be S-O-N) meaning a child,
A living child, not merely pleasure's leap,
Would be the consummation of your lust.
Your wit thus proving your genetic worth,
She'd take you in her willing arms at last.
  And, Andrew, I'm no different than you are;
I'd like to be assured (if I'm correct
In sensing some concealed anxiety
In the bravura of your argument)
I'd be the picture father of her child—
No, not her child alone, but mine as well,
My answer to the jaws of gnawing time
For, by my troth, and you should tell her so,
She certainly is passing beautiful.

BOUNTY

Venus within the sickle of the moon
Above the snow-streaked mountain range—
Not likely in our lifetime to repeat,
Though I can cradle it in memory.

I watch the planet in our arc of moon,
Making its rounds, as everyone must do,
So that on this rotating earth we live
Not just in fact but also in the mind,

And everything I witness is my own design
My seeing makes of variations on
The theme of mountains in reflected light
Or the blue ocean sliding in its hues.

And when I stroll along the slushing tide,
Feeling the flow, the sand-suck, the dull rasp
Of pebbles at my toes, I see myself
Outside myself, I see my life revolving

Through the gleam of your believing eyes,
My life merged inextricably with yours,
As likewise you have known yourself through me—
The moon with Venus in its crescent arms.

Before conceiving, as mind says we must,
Our being gone, we apprehend that we're alive,
And thus we harvest sight so precious life
Must spend itself to make such bounty thrive.

DISTRACTION

        What consolation can I bring
    from thinking of the unity
of cosmic law
        to the hard fact the universe
    is still expanding
in displays of swirling light
        from its hot Big Bang origin
    and *will* in time, not *might*,
collapse upon itself
        because of ample gravity
    in what we call Big Crunch
or will thin out forever so,
        eventually, nothing alive,
    intelligent or self-aware,
will manage to survive?
        Yes, everything we now hold precious—
    science, art, our codes of sympathy—
will then be lost beyond recall,
        and holy truthfulness requires
    that we acknowledge loss as absolute,
that fleetingness is all.
        And yet, are thoughts like these
    merely avoidances
of losses more immediate:
        my brother's cancer,
    which the stellar crab commemorates;
my sister's heart attack

while visiting the planetarium?
  The hot-cold options of apocalypse—
which somehow we have always known
    are certain—they are all
    we have, and must be faced.
"There can be no
    nobility in our avoiding them!"
I blurt these words out like a fool
and thus surprise myself,
    walking to school
    to lecture on the solace
of impersonal reflection, thought,
    indifferent to human tears,
    as I have done,
like a detached observing eye,
    for over forty years.
  But I'm distracted
by a girl in a red woolen hat
    who seems more beautiful
    than lawful nature need contrive,
peddling her silver scooter toward
    a local destination I can't know.
  She's also taken by surprise
in hearing someone elderly like me
    who's talking to himself out loud;
    she almost bumps into a tree.
"Sorry!" I call out to her
    as she swerves away.
  And I can picture her—I see
her lips, her cheeks, her hat—
    speeding day after designated day
    beyond the Dipper and Orion's belt
to nowhere that conceivably
    is meaningful to humankind,
    diminishing and fading out

into some dimming galaxy,
  yet self-absorbed, with no distress
 that can distract
or separate her from herself,
  not even her own lovely face,
 except my inadvertent outcry,
"Sorry!" hurtling through the emptiness, the blur
  of blue, engulfing space,
 a cry I can't take back, that streaks
like a white icy comet after her.

BULLFROG SONATA

for Bill Zaranka

In the Montana moonlight where
My urgent croaking pulses loud and long
And echoes with the pungent air
To demonstrate my genes are strong,
The proud frog princess will appear to me
And she'll inspire a spawning spree.

She does not know why she responds,
And my competitors are vexed to see
Of all the wooers in our pond
The most successful one is me,
But maybe I am foolish to explore
Why they have less and I have more.

What worthiness in me, my song,
Makes me deserving in some vast design,
Beyond whatever's right or wrong,
As if the pond were wholly mine,
So that my princess willingly concurs
In sharing with me what is hers?

I'm sorry, guys, that's how things go,
That's how it's been, how it will always be;
You can sing harder but you know
Nothing will change, nothing can free
You from whatever makes you what you are,
So you must envy from afar.

I'm sure there is no fathoming
God's plan for how the universe is run,
Why some must weep and some may sing,
Some halted before life's begun.
But I grow weary of this mystery—
It's time to start a spawning spree.

REPLY OF THE FROG PRINCESS

Let's first admit: he sure can sing,
That big guy squatting on the lily pad,
Though I'm not taken with his reasoning;
His arrogance, though innocently bad,
May serve our future progeny—
And so I'm ready for a spawning spree.

I doubt he's even read *The Origin,*
Though self-awareness is of little use
Since we're fixed by how we begin
And knowledge brings its own abuse;
In singing all he really needs to know
Is how to float his loud notes' flow.

He's not the kind to stick around,
But if my sons resemble him
The other ladies of the pond are bound,
Beyond what may appear no more than whim,
To let impassioned singing win the day
And play the part he'd have them play.

I guess that's how things have to go,
And that design works well enough for me,
So what more do I need to know,
Since through acceptance I feel free,
Though there are lots of guys out there
Who have no chance to make it anywhere.

That troubles me, I'm not sure why,
For one can't help but see and, seeing, feel,
How many songs beneath the arching sky
Are wasted, though there's no appeal
For changing things that old, so you'll agree
It's time to start a spawning spree.

REMAINS

Ageless and vague, your face remains
For me to conjure up. I can recall
You underneath this willow tree,
Right here where I stand now
To watch the flutter of your vanishing,

As if your being gone were something solid
That a long-grown child could touch—
Your cheek, your arm. I can recall,
As if eternal in their vanishing,
Your features whose pale blur remains

As long as I can think of vanishing
As something like an autumn tree that's here,
Moving in place at the slight touch
Of hazy air, though fervent green is gone
And your last words are now beyond recall.

Why then should I exert the effort to hold on
When even memory is vanishing
And the blank sense of what is gone,
Your veined, small hands, suffuses what is here,
A space of absence that remains,

So that when I reach out to touch
The rough bark of the willow tree
As evidence that something still remains,

I am reminded freshly that you're gone,
Recalling what I barely can recall,

Your round face vivid in its vanishing.
Your touch no longer here, the whitened air
Of your dissolving look remains to dwell upon
And make your face seem fresh—the lost,
Eternal face of what is gone.

DEFIANCE

How well then can defiance serve?
    Can I argue the wind into retreat?
The wheeling red-tailed hawk, does he
    find purpose somewhere
in his predatory brain, breaking the circle
    of his yellow-eyed descent?
And does the spider spinning from her gut
    enjoy the web she fabricates
simply because such weaving is her own
    and satisfies a hunger
no less urgent than the swallowed fly?
    Pausing beside the lily pond
of random yellow, random white, can I
    not will that image to suffice
as motivation to endure?
    Merely the word *sufficient*
still might help, for how did expectation
    start its fantasy of kindness
to assuage the bitterness that bites my lips
    for suffering we add
to pain already inescapable?
    Even evoking *kindness* tells me
I'm still wishing what I've deemed unwishable.
    So let me concentrate
on what I see, not what thought adds:
    the hawk as he rebuffs the wind

to seek some rabbit as his prey; the spider
    looking like a dewdrop
in its web; bullfrog concealing green
    of gleaming lily pads.
They are all simply there, the fact of them,
    as if such unconsidered sights
might make acceptable a world
    that's ignorantly cruel,
ignorantly beautiful, a wordless world
    to innocently offer you
as a late wedding gift that's fit
    to set against the windy void,
had I some kinder power to sweeten it.

RIPENESS

  Maybe before he wrote it down,
      Shakespeare declaimed out loud,
"Ripeness is all!" as if
      for that immortal instant
he inhabited a world
      of his own making. But
in that moment of his worded breath,
      one million billion billion atoms were
flung free into the universal air,
      and so the likelihood is that
I, here and now, must have inhaled
      a few of them, some dusty grains
of what great empathetic Shakespeare might
      have meant by ripeness, some
abundant season of the mind
      my straining mind
might name and harvest as its own.
      I know forgetfulness
won't qualify as ripeness:
      take my aged mother
who does not recall her husband died
      three years ago. And yet
my knowledge she no longer knows,
      yes, that might qualify,
my resolute awareness nothing
      can restore her sense of self

that once could contemplate
    the loved ones she had lost
and find black loss acceptable because—
    because no other choice
can maintain sanity. One can contrive
    to take necessity
as if, to take possession of one's life,
    one willed oneself to will
each circumstance one suffered from.
    Like August drought
that desiccates the stunted fields
    and makes the forests tinder
for the unassuaging fires, Nature
    must have her way—there is
no fruitful arguing with that, no matter
    how grim that may seem.
And yet I cannot help but feel
    true ripeness might connote
some sense of sweetened thought
    available to all, some atom
from the lexicon of what life's bounty gives
    and dying takes away,
Say like the *p* in ripeness or the *p*
    in Shakespeare's name,
the letter we might choose to signify
    prolific life—*p* as in peach,
or plum, or pear, or apricot,
    or apple with its double *p*s;
I've got a *p* in my name too. I watch
    my thoughts drift off
into an alphabet of wistfulness
    because I can't find ripeness
in my mother's deepening demise
    or my contrivance of necessity

redeemed as choice. And yet
    the overwhelming sweetness
of sweet Shakespeare's words,
    the mystery of what he meant,
lightens my mind and makes the lilting air,
    although impersonal, still good
to grasp and gather in the lungs,
    so that it might appear
some plenitude of ripeness, even only
    of ripe words, might still
occur at any moment, anywhere.

GHOSTS

And do the ghosts themselves die out,
Expiring imperceptibly
As one by one their lives' regrets, the sense
By which each knew himself,
Diminish to inconsequence?

Hardly to be distinguished from the life
His father lived, a man
Who pondered the repeating waves
And then one windless day did not return,
Will his ghost tell his story to himself?

If he can picture where he went a grief ago,
The scene might help him hold on, not forget—
Perhaps him sitting by a waterfall
Or on a rotting log where he once watched
Bright snow-tipped mountains through dark trees—

And save him from dissolving into air.
If only he could make his memory
Recall the day his father disappeared,
He could allow himself to improvise
Fresh details to renew the fading past—

His mother's vein-blue strand of beads,
Details embellished as a way of holding on.
He needs to keep his melancholy fresh

So that fresh loss inspires belief that he
Somehow remains ecstatically alive,

Still filled with longing to be understood
As if, of all the dead, he were unique
Merely by having gazed upon the cresting sea
Or sunset on a purple mountain peak.
Yet maybe I confuse the father with the son;

Maybe, though new to death, already
He's content just fading out, content at last
Relinquishing the willow tree he climbed
Against his father's rules, descending
Slowly branch by golden branch

Into forbidden evening light,
Into unmoving air replete with quietude,
So even his own mother's calling voice
Becomes a thinning shadow of a shade,
A wisp of time from which a ghost is made.

SHOWDOWN

Is it not time to make some synthesis?
    Have not sufficient years passed by?
I stand, like my preceding fathers, by the great abyss,
    the chasm of steep edges and of
        clashing clouds like breaking waves,
With no food to sustain myself
    but revelation that there's nothing
        yet to be revealed,
Just emptiness that fills blank emptiness
    and absences compounding absences,
The multitudes of stars receding,
    atoms spinning in the orbit
        of their own uncertainties.
Why am I then not more aghast
    at such conditions so impersonal?
Why do my hands not cover up my mouth,
    clasped closed in fear of blasphemy?
Is it because there's no one to respond,
    no one to care or to apologize?
Have I not banished my accusers
    from the courtroom of my mind?
What can they say to me that I have not
    heard myself say so many times?
The rampant wind takes no chastisement
    from attendant rain; the flooded stream
        does not rebuke itself.

Nothing requires a judgment need be made
    that life should strive to be
        other than what it is:
The eagle with a fish arced in its beak;
    the slug that goes on being just a slug.
The rocket waiting to be launched
    appropriates the sun; it knows
It is no more than mere assembled light,
    yet it demands my reverence—
An idol needing its idolaters, a temple
    waiting to be filled with song.
Surely, if hope is to be found, it must
    be found right here; this oceanfront
        must constitute its place.
Yet will not hope, long after our own planet
    has burned out, sucked back into the sun,
Arrive somewhere to start again,
    again with pioneers of consciousness,
To seed life where no life had been
    as if purpose were to be discovered
        in evolving dust?
Maybe we'll get it better on a second try,
    or, maybe, counting Noah's flood,
A third try or a fourth—for why assume we are
    more than a trial run,
        a vast, extravagant experiment?
Although our sorrows seem escapable—
    as if their causes could be redesigned,
Removed as accidents: the driver,
    sleeping at the wheel, awake;
The romping kids, who failed to test the ice,
    be warned and made aware in time,
How can we change what in our hearts we are,
    no freer than the laws of energy:

The jealous knife jerked upwards in the dark;
    the lie that grips down to the very bone?
And who shall teach the gods whose love requires
    grim hatred of all other gods to be true
        to their loving selves?
So who am I to synthesize a vow
    that can transform me as I am?
And who am I to make whole
    what profusion has made disparate,
From aardvark, baboon, through to zebra
    with the human alphabet between?
Still unassuaged remains ancestral lust
    for killing just to stay alive and live.
No matter how we try to reinvent ourselves
    through sacrifice, becoming what our wills
        intend, we recognize
Devouring emptiness in waves of dread,
    although our wives, our parents, children, friends,
Mean quite enough to break our hearts
    or give sweet sustenance like bread.